MATH IN THE REAL WORLD OF DESIGN AND ART

Geometry, Measurements, and Projections

by Shirley Cook

Incentive Publications, Inc.
Nashville, Tennessee

Illustrated by Kathleen Bullock
Cover by Geoffrey Brittingham
Edited by Anna Quinn
ISBN 0-86530-344-4

PRINTED IN THE UNITED STATES OF AMERICA

Table of Contents

Preface

Long before the National Council for Teaching Mathematics standards were released, teachers knew the importance of making learning meaningful to students. The standards reinforced the idea that teachers need to help students become problem solvers by linking math to the real world and to other areas of the curriculum. For students, numbers should be more than mere figures on the page—they should represent solutions to real-life situations and problems.

Math in the Real World of Design and Art focuses on real-world links while helping students to refine problem-solving skills. The culminating activity—construction of a model Geo-Lab—draws these skills together with a product-oriented project that also serves as a math assessment.

Students will become involved with studies of two-dimensional and three-dimensional geometric shapes; properties of angles, triangles, quadrilaterals, and polygons; symmetry; measurement; perimeter; area; volume; tessellations; and pentominoes. Each section stands alone for mini lessons or flexible grouping instruction. Students may work in teams, pairs, or independently throughout the course of the unit.

Several artistic projects are integrated with the math as geometry lends itself naturally to art. Students will have an opportunity to create original tessellations and three-dimensional figures of unusual shape as well as geometric quilt patterns and tiling designs.

In the Planning Log, students organize their work and involve their peers in the solution of problems as they create a model of the Geo-Lab. It also helps them evaluate the group experience and incorporate writing into the math experience.

Math in the Real World of Design and Art provides a hands-on learning experience in an authentic mathematics environment.

The Geo-Lab

Students working on the Geo-Lab will be involved in creative problem solving while using geometric concepts and measuring skills to create a product model.

In teams of three or four, students will form companies that will design a special math laboratory that could be purchased by their school district to further the study of mathematics. Design requirements are stated in the Planning Log. A model of the lab will then be created by each team using newspaper dowels. Directions for the construction of the dowels are found in the Planning Log.

The project should be completed within seven work periods. The length of time may be modified to fit your schedule. As you oversee the project, you will control the supply of dowels and tape. The following guidelines are offered to make the project run more smoothly.

- Students may purchase dowels from you only three times. Encourage them to plan carefully. They may use tape at any time and then estimate their total use at the end and record the expense in their expense log.

- Geo-Lab structures will be judged on sturdiness, appropriateness to the task, originality, visual appeal, and innovative features.

- Presentations will be judged on preparation, clarity of speech, involvement of all members of the company, accuracy of records, quality of brochure, and journal preparation.

- At the end of the project, students will be asked to fill out an evaluation of their participation.

Vocabulary

1. Circle: .... a continuous closed curved line, every point of which is equally distant from the center
2. Cone: .... a solid figure that narrows to a point from a circular base
3. Cube: .... a solid figure with six equal square sides
4. Cylinder: .... a solid geometric figure that has two parallel sides that are circles
5. Diamond: .... a plane figure with four equal sides, two acute angles, and two obtuse angles
6. Polygon: .... a closed plane figure with at least three straight lines (for example, a square is a polygon)
7. Polyhedra: .... a closed solid figure made by joining plane polygons; each two adjoining polygons have a common edge
8. Prism: .... a solid figure having two equal and parallel faces with other faces that are parallelograms
9. Pyramid: .... a solid figure with a polygon base and triangular sides that intersect at a point
10. Rectangle: .... a four-sided plane figure with opposite sides which are equal and parallel
11. Sphere: .... a round, solid figure, all surface points of which are at an equal distance from the center
12. Square: .... a four-sided plane figure with all sides of equal length and four 90 degree angles
13. Symmetry: .... patterns that are identical on either side of a line
14. Tessellation: .... a pattern that repeats itself within a defined area without overlapping or leaving any undefined space
15. Trapezoid: .... a four-sided plane figure with only two sides parallel
16. Triangle: .... a plane figure that has three sides and three angles
17. Vertex: .... the point of intersection of the sides of an angle (plural: vertices)

Exploring Angles

Two lines that meet at a common point create an angle. The point at which they meet is called the vertex.

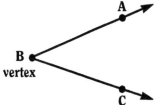

An angle is measured in degrees. Around the vertex there are 360 degrees.

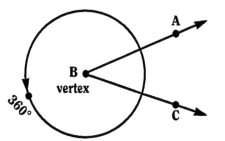

An angle can be named in three ways—two by identifying the vertex and both of its points (the vertex is always named in the center, but the points can be in any order), and one by identifying the vertex alone. For example, the angle above can be named <ABC, <CBA, or <B.

Look at each angle shown below and give three names for each one.

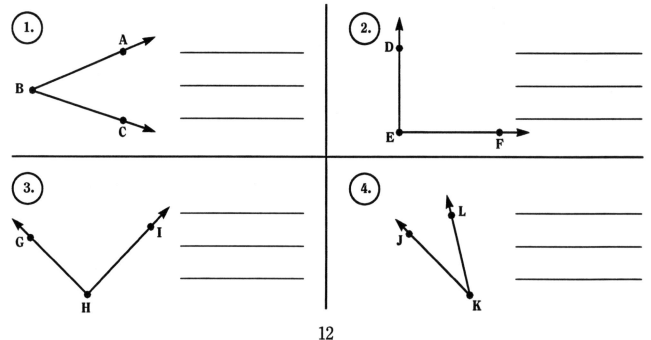

12

Interior Angles

When three line segments have been used to create a triangle, three angles are formed inside the triangle. These are called interior angles. When the three interior angles of a triangle are added together, their sum always equals 180 degrees.

If we know the measure of two of the interior angles of a triangle, we can find the measure of the third angle. For example:

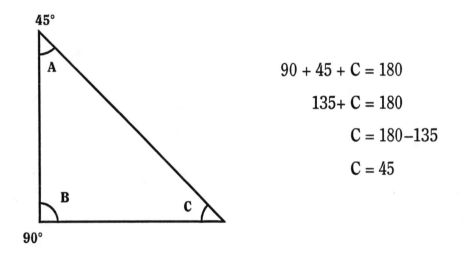

$$90 + 45 + C = 180$$
$$135 + C = 180$$
$$C = 180 - 135$$
$$C = 45$$

Find the missing angle in each of the following problems. Set up an equation to solve for the measure of the missing angle in each problem.

1. If <ABC = 90° and <BAC = 45°, what is the measure of <BCA?

2. If <ACB = 100° and <CAB = 45°, what is the measure of <ABC?

3. If <FDE = 135° and <DEF = 17°, what is the measure of <EFD?

4. If <RST = 60° and <STR = 60°, what is the measure of <TRS?

5. If <LMN = 105° and <MNL = 42°, what is the measure of <NLM?

Exploring Two Dimensions with Right Triangles

A triangle is a three-sided figure. The sides join to form vertices. When the interior angles of the triangle are added together, their sum equals 180 degrees.

These are right triangles.

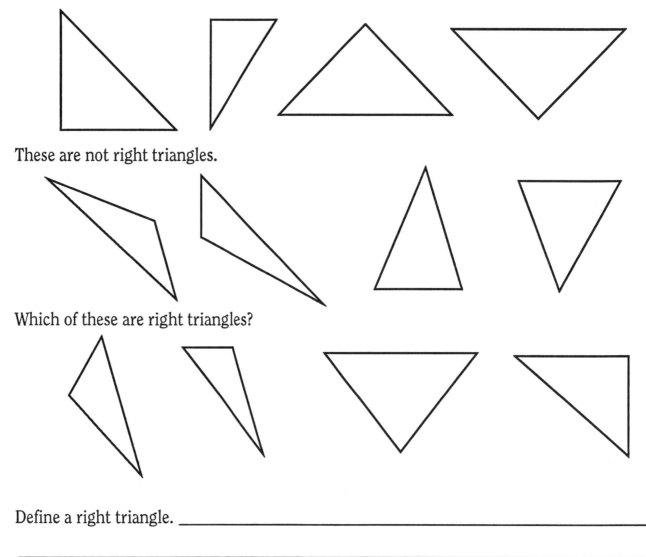

These are not right triangles.

Which of these are right triangles?

Define a right triangle. _____

_____

_____

Math in the Real World of Design and Art

Exploring Two Dimensions with Obtuse Triangles

A triangle is a three-sided figure. The sides join to form vertices. When the interior angles of the triangle are added together, their sum equals 180 degrees.

These are obtuse triangles.

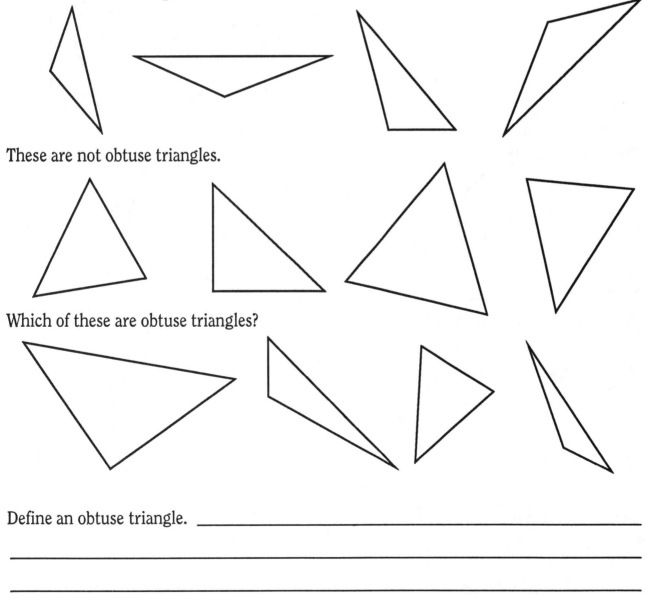

These are not obtuse triangles.

Which of these are obtuse triangles?

Define an obtuse triangle. _____

_____

_____

15

Exploring Two Dimensions with Scalene Triangles

A triangle is a three-sided figure. The sides join to form vertices. When the interior angles of the triangle are added together, their sum equals 180 degrees.

These are scalene triangles.

These are not scalene triangles.

Which of these are scalene triangles?

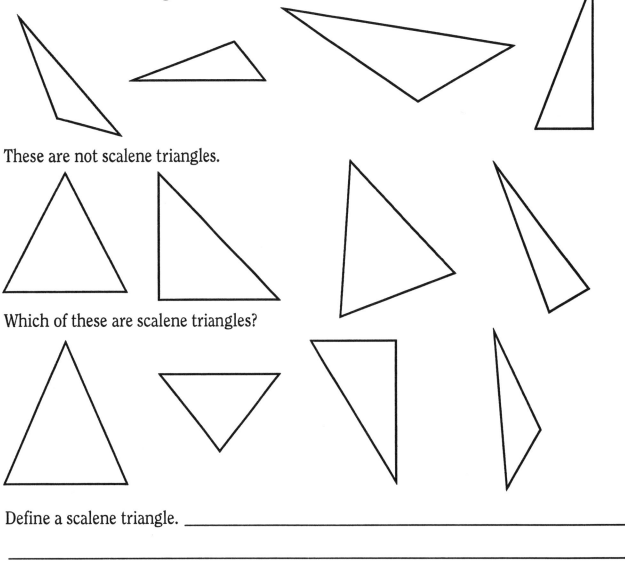

Define a scalene triangle. _____

_____

_____

16

Triangle Truths

Using one-inch wide strips of construction paper, create each of the following triangles. Tape the edges together.

1. 4" x 4" x 4"

2. 4" x 9" x 5"

3. 8" x 8" x 8"

4. 4" x 8" x 3"

5. 7" x 4" x 7"

6. 6" x 7" x 4"

7. 5" x 5" x 8"

8. 2" x 9" x 4"

You have been asked to write a news article for the local paper detailing the discovery that you have made about triangles. Write your article here:

_____

_____

_____

_____

_____

_____

_____

A Triangle Divided

Divide each triangle into equal parts as directed.

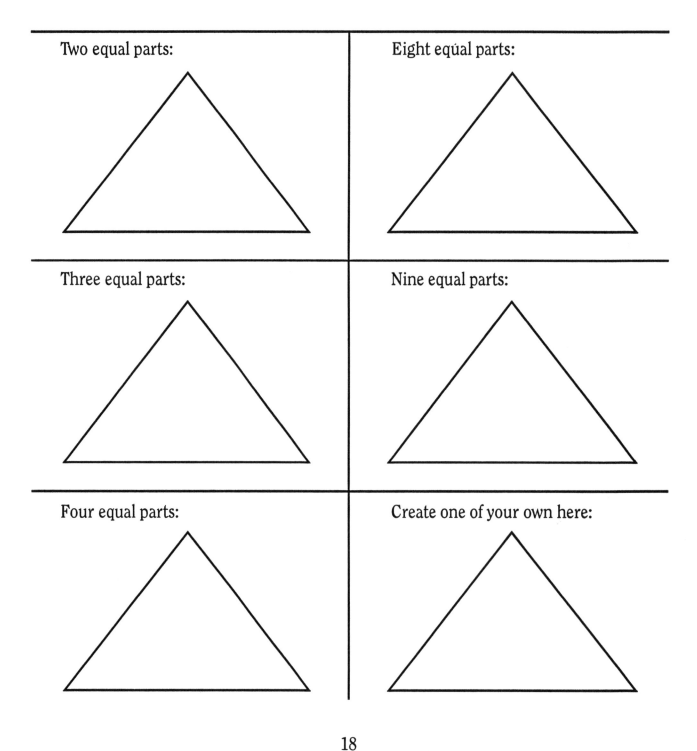

Two equal parts:

Eight equal parts:

Three equal parts:

Nine equal parts:

Four equal parts:

Create one of your own here:

Math in the Real World of Design and Art

Two-Dimensional Figures

Polygons are closed figures that lie in a plane and have at least three straight lines as sides. Each of the polygons below has its own name which relates to the number of sides.

Research to discover:
1. The name of each figure
2. The number of diagonals that can traverse each figure from one vertex to another

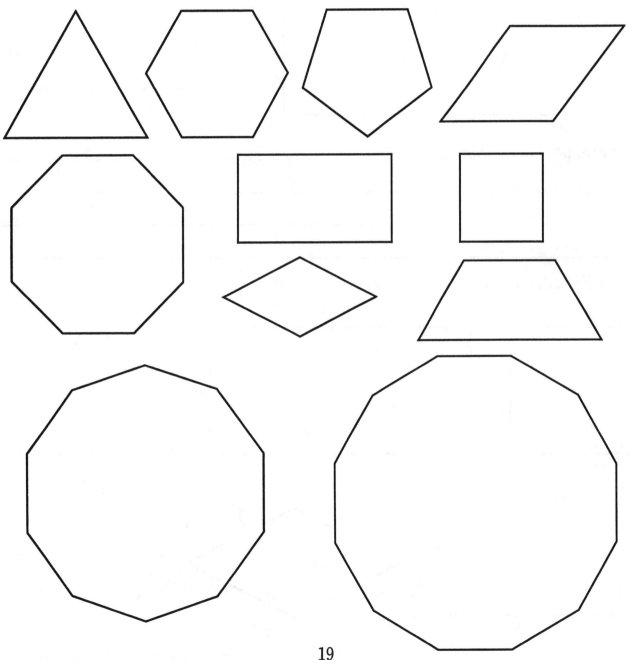

19

Math in the Real World of Design and Art

Working with Polygons

A two-dimensional figure that has three or more straight sides is called a polygon. Polygons include such shapes as squares, rectangles, triangles, and hexagons.

The perimeter of each of the following polygons is 100 feet:

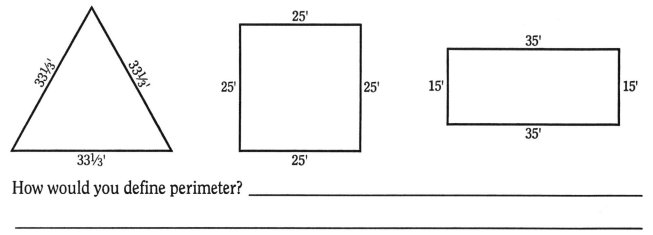

How would you define perimeter? _____

_____

_____

_____

Find the perimeter of each of the following polygons.

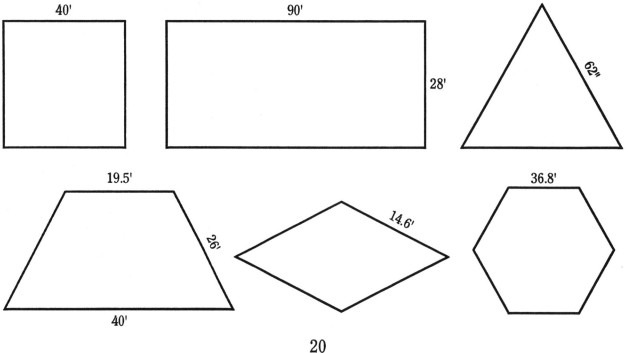

Mix it Up

Trace and cut out the shapes on the left. Arrange them so that the congruent sides match, and create new shapes in the boxes on the right.

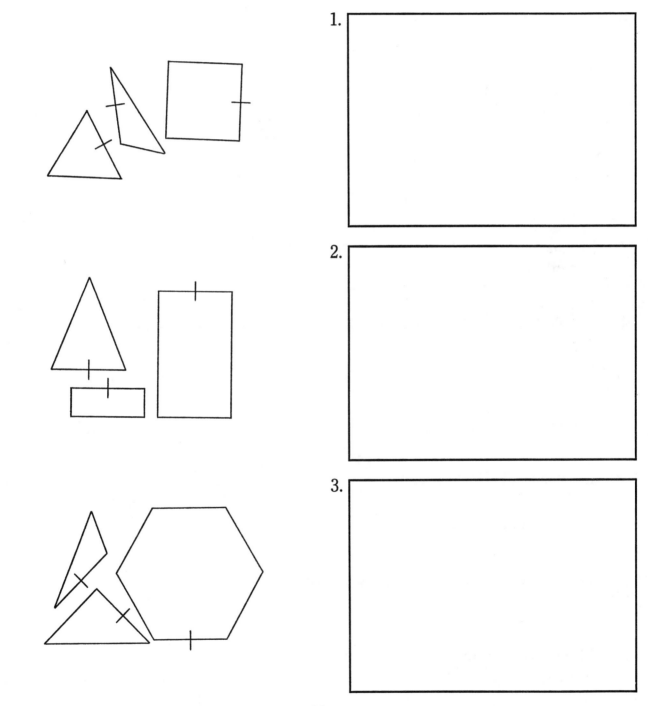

1.

2.

3.

Which Is Which?

A quadrilateral is a closed figure with four straight sides. Quadrilaterals include parallelograms, trapezoids, rectangles, squares, rhombuses, and diamonds.

Tell which type(s) of quadrilateral(s) are described in each of the following situations and write the answer on the line.

1. Sides across from one another are congruent   _____

2. This quadrilateral has more than one right angle   _____

3. A shape with more than one line of symmetry   _____

4. This quadrilateral is rotationally symmetrical (turn of less than 360 degrees)   _____

5. All sides of this shape are congruent   _____

6. The diagonals of this shape bisect each other   _____

7. Adjacent sides of this shape are congruent   _____

8. All opposing sides are parallel   _____

9. This shape has only one set of parallel sides   _____

10. This shape has two pairs of opposite angles that are equal   _____

11. This quadrilateral has no line of symmetry   _____

Working with Circles

A circle is a round, flat shape with a line circling a center point that is always at an equal distance from the center.

The circumference is the distance around the outer edge of the circle. To find this distance, mathematicians use the formula $C = \pi d$. The value of π (the Greek letter pi, pronounced "pie") is 3.14; the d in the formula is the diameter. Diameter is found by measuring the length of a straight line that passes from one side of the circle to the other while passing through the center point.

The area of the circle is found by using the formula $A = \pi r^2$. The radius (r) is half of the diameter or the distance from the center point to the edge of the circle.

Answer the following questions.

1. If the new city park had a flower garden with a diameter of 10 feet, what would be the circumference of the garden?

2. What would be the area of the flower garden?

3. What is the diameter of a circular area that has a radius of 27.3 feet?

4. The beautifully carved carousel in the park has a radius of seven feet. What is the circumference?

5. When would it be important for people to be able to find the circumference or area of a circle?

23

Math in the Real World of Design and Art

Valuable Circles

We make use of circles every day when we handle coins. How much do you know about coins, though? Why do you think they are circular in shape? Using a penny, a nickel, a quarter, and a ruler, solve the following problems.

1. If you wanted to make a three-dimensional structure using pennies, what could you do?

2. How many pennies would be stacked together to make a cylinder two inches long?

3. How many pennies would be stacked together to make a rod 1 foot in height?

   100 feet?

   1 mile?

4. What is the circumference of a quarter?

5. What is the circumference of a nickel?

24

Math in the Real World of Design and Art

Floral Fantasy

Use a compass to create seven overlapping circles. What is the least number of colors you can use to color your floral fantasy so that no adjoining sections are of the same color? Color your creation with the least number of colors possible.

Creative Coinage

A contest has been organized to have a new coin created. It would not take the place of any of our current coins, but it would function as a needed piece of money in our current system of exchange.

Before beginning your design work, think about the importance of your task. What amount of money will your new coin represent and why? What type of metal will your new coin be made of? Will your new coin be usable in places like vending machines? How will other businesses have to change to accommodate use of your new coin?

Draw your coin below. You may use any type of polygon in its design. Write a paragraph of information justifying your design and its function in everyday life.

Math in the Real World of Design and Art

Circling the Globe

1. Around the globe we can observe vastly different types of architecture. In many parts of Europe, for example, the architecture is quite ornate and includes a wide variety of geometric shapes. In non-industrialized nations the architecture is relatively simple. In the United States, there is a wide variety of styles that range from fairly simple to rather ornate.

If you could design the home of your dreams, what would it look like?

On another sheet of paper, create a blueprint (floorplan) of a home that you think would be perfect for your family. What geometric forms have you used in your blueprint?

2. If you lived in a non-industrialized part of the world, you would have to take great care to create the most structure with the least amount of materials. Using a 10-inch string and the graph paper provided, create as many different figures as possible that have a perimeter of 10 inches. As you place your string on the graph paper, trace around it. Then determine the area of each structure and fill in the chart below.

Figure	Shape	Area
1		_____
2		_____
3		_____
4		_____
5		_____

What conclusions can you draw about shape and area? _____

_____

_____

Geometry and Art

Research an artist who relied heavily on geometric form to create his or her artwork. Write a brief paragraph about him or her. Be sure to mention at least two of his or her pieces of art. What geometric shapes are in these pieces?

_____

_____

_____

_____

_____

_____

_____

_____

_____

_____

In the space below, create a drawing that is entirely geometric.

What Kind of Shape Are We In?

Certain objects have had the same geometric shape for many years. This may be due to the appropriateness of the shape; the lack of time, money, or energy needed to make design changes; time-honored tradition that is not based on need; or other considerations.

Look at the items listed below. Decide if the geometric shape of the object is appropriate or if it would be in the product's best interest to change the shape. If the shape needs to be changed, how should the new product look? Defend your decisions for or against change in each case.

Product	Current Shape	New Shape	Reasons
License Plate			
Dollar Bill			
Pencil/Pen			
Writing Paper			
Television			
Classroom			
Ice Cream Cone			
Arrow			
Hockey Puck			

Repeating Identical Patterns

When a particular shape or group of shapes is repeated over and over again in such a manner that an entire surface is covered without having any blank space or any of the pattern overlap, a tessellation is created. Draw the figure below on the grid so that the entire surface of the grid is covered without overlapping the figure onto itself or leaving any open space on the grid.

Math in the Real World of Design and Art

To Tessellate or Not to Tessellate

Which of the following geometric figures will tessellate? Give an example of each tessellation on the grid provided.

1.

2.

3.

4.

5.

6.

7.

8.

Tessellating Two-Dimensional Figures

1. Cut one or two polygons from a piece of 4" x 4" construction paper. In the area below create a design that repeats itself without overlapping onto itself. This careful repetition of a pattern is known as a tessellation.

2. Create a triangular tessellation on the dot grid below.

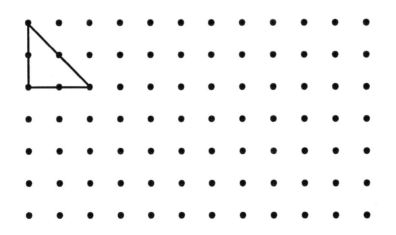

Tessellating, page two

3. Create a tessellating polygon on the dot grid below.

Math in the Real World of Design and Art

Patterns

Tessellating, page 3

4. Create a rectangular tessellation on the dot grid below.

Math in the Real World of Design and Art

Tessellating, page 4

5. Create a tessellating quadrilateral on the dot grid below.

Tiling a Gazebo

The city council has asked your construction company to provide a gazebo in the new park that it is constructing. They want the gazebo to be a place where people can sit and watch the wildlife in the area. Their instructions are to put a tiled floor in the gazebo. They want the tiling to be done following these specifications:

1. There should be at least three colors used in the tiles
2. The tiling pattern should incorporate three polygons that tessellate
3. The final floor should remind the patrons of the park in spring

Create a sample of the tile pattern that you plan to tessellate in the area below. Color it as you would like the pattern to look. (On a piece of graph paper you may choose to make a more complete sample of the tile as it tessellates across the floor.)

The Problem with Pentominoes

A pentomino is a two-dimensional shape made from five squares, each of which has at least one side in common with another square. This is a pentomino:

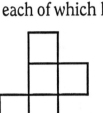
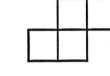

Can you draw the other eleven on the graph paper below?

Challenge: Can you cut around any of the pentomino perimeters and create a three-dimensional structure from the material? Share this activity with a classmate.

Can you tessellate a pentomino? Try it on a piece of graph paper.

37

Creating with Pentominoes

Use the twelve pentominoes to create a rectangle. Cut out each pentomino carefully. Then place the pentominoes together as you would a puzzle to create a rectangle. When you have created the rectangle, glue it onto a piece of paper. Share your results.

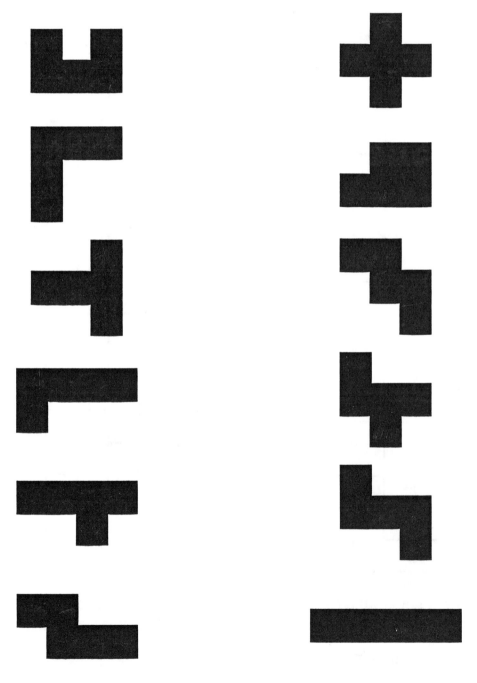

Symmetrical/Asymmetrical

Using the dotted line as a centerpoint, determine if each figure is symmetrical or asymmetrical. Then label it correctly.

39

Complete the Picture

Complete each picture to create a symmetrical figure.

Symmetry Activity

People in advertising and education often need to produce large letters of the alphabet for posters or bulletin boards. Today, this work may be done with a computer or a cutter. However, if the letters need to be made of special materials such as fabric or heavy paper, the person doing the creating must find a way to make large letters without the aid of patterns or stencils.

Fortunately, many of the letters of the alphabet are symmetrical. For example, if a student folds his or her paper in half vertically, they can easily design and cut out the letter A. Folding the paper in half horizontally can create a letter B.

Decide which letters of the alphabet can be created using horizontal folds and which can be created using vertical folds. List them in the appropriate space. Are there letters that use a combination of horizontal and vertical folds?

Horizontal Folds:

Vertical Folds:

Combinations:

Try cutting out several of the letters. Tell about the most difficult letter that you tried. Why was it difficult?

_____

_____

_____

41

Symmetrical and Sophisticated

You have recently been hired by a prominent fashion designer to create some innovative new fashions. She wants you to use any colors that you think will be "hot" in the marketplace. She wants you to design an entire ensemble for a person of your age, sex, and build. There is only one stipulation—your fashions must all be symmetrical in cut and design. That way, each garment can be cut from one piece of fabric that is properly folded.

Example:

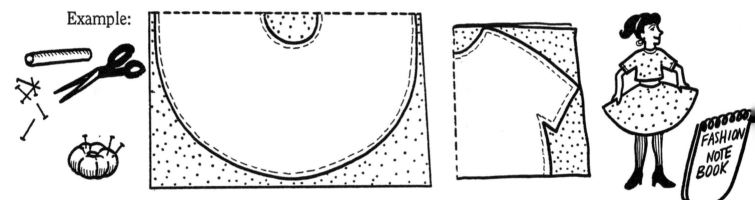

Use a piece of paper to fold and cut an example of each type of designer clothing that you create. (You must create at least two pieces to form your ensemble.) After you have created each piece, pattern it partially or completely using a symmetrical design. Your design must be created entirely from geometric shapes.

Sketch your geometric pattern here:

An Asymmetrical Point of View

We all know of celebrities who prefer to be different in the way they dress. You have been hired by one of the biggest promotional agencies in the world. One of their best clients wants an entirely new look. They want a two-piece ensemble suitable for a man or a woman that is not symmetrical in any way.

Both the construction and the patterning of the garment must be asymmetrical.

Sketch your design ideas below.

43

Symmetry

Geometric Quilting

Create a symmetrical quilt design using only geometric shapes. You may use only four colors to enhance the design.

Solving the Paper-Folding Mysteries

Look carefully at each of the pieces of folded paper. The cutouts on each page are symmetrical. Next to each folded page, draw the page as you think it would appear when it is unfolded.

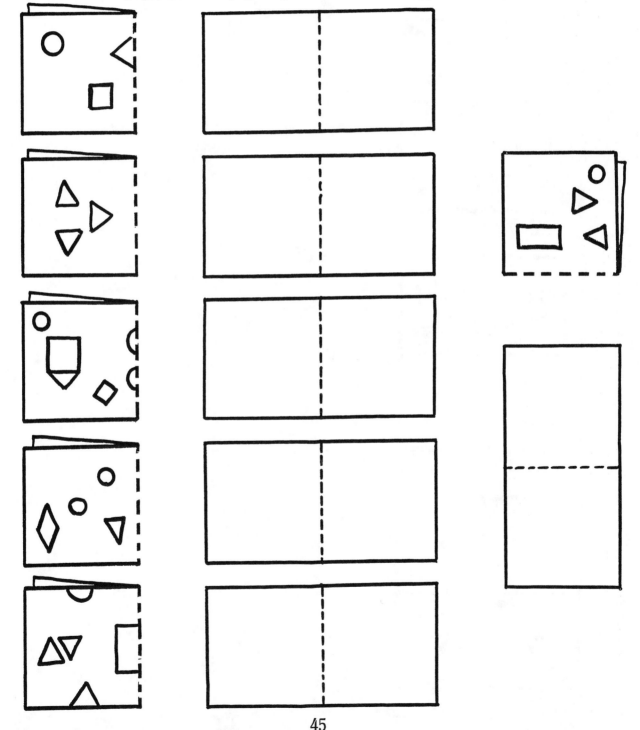

45

Math in the Real World of Design and Art

Symmetry

More Paper-Folding Mysteries

Each of the following pieces of unfolded paper will be folded into fourths. Next to each one show how the papers will look once they are folded.

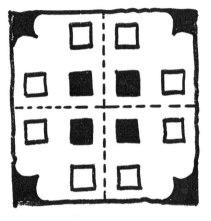

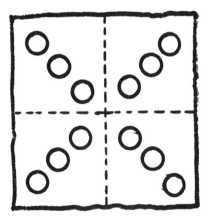

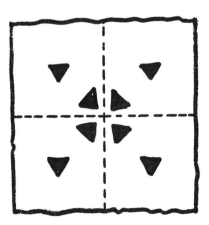

Paper Folding with a Different Twist

Using one square piece of paper, you can create a three-dimensional cube. Follow the directions carefully.

1. Begin with a square piece of paper of any size. The edge of the cube you create will be one-fourth of the length of one side of the square.

2. Fold the paper from corner to corner. Open and fold across the center.

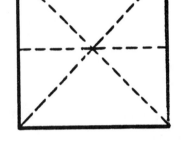

3. Fold the paper as shown in figure C.

4. Fold the front of AB down to point C.

5. Do the same for the back corners, F and G.

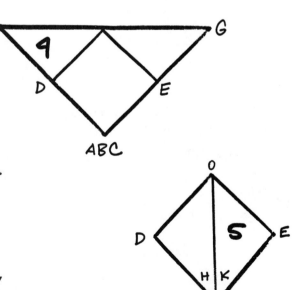

47

Symmetry

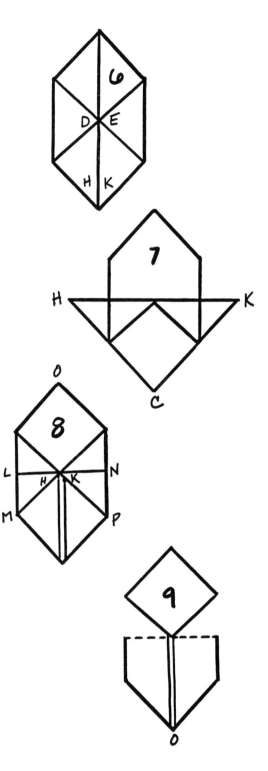

6. The corners on sides D and E are now double. Fold the corners D and E to meet in the center. Turn the square over and do the same on the back.

7. One end will now be free of loose corners. Fold the loose corners on the opposite end (H and K) out on the front to form G.

8. Fold H and K in to the center. Do the same with the points on the back.

9. Open the folds D and E and tuck the triangles LHM and KNP into the pockets of D and E. Do this for both sides.

10. Blow sharply into the small hole at O. This will inflate your cube. Crease the edges to create a finished cube.

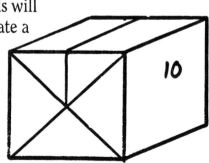

48

Overlapping Shapes

Look at the shapes below. Draw the way they would look if the following directions were followed exactly.

1. Place the circle on the rectangle.

2. Overlap the rectangle and the triangle with the triangle being on the bottom.

Color the following sets of shapes to show how they would look if they were overlapped according to the directions given.

1.

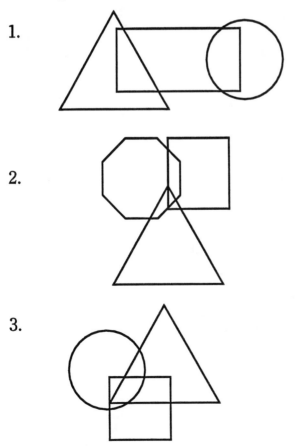

Shade to make the rectangle appear to be on the bottom.

2.

Shade to make the octagon appear to be in the center of the stack.

3.

Shade to make the square appear to be on the bottom and the triangle appear to be on the top.

49

Geometric Analogies

For each set of figures, draw the figure that will complete the analogy.

1.

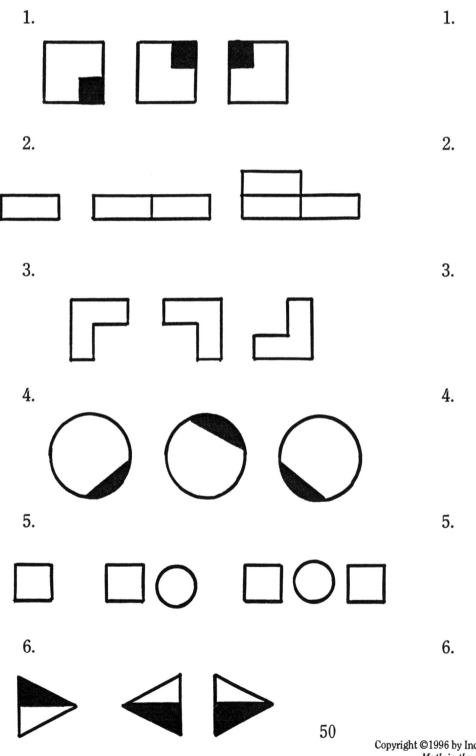

1.

2.

2.

3.

3.

4.

4.

5.

5.

6.

6.

50

Turn About Is Fair Play

Draw each figure as it would look after being turned 90 degrees.

Draw each figure as it would look after being turned 180 degrees.

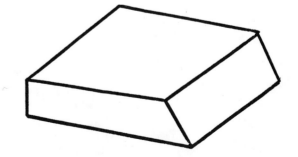

51

Measurement Review

Measure the following lines in inches, centimeters, and millimeters. Record your findings on each line segment.

1. _____

2. _____

3. _____

Measure the lengths of the following figures in inches, centimeters, and millimeters. Record your findings below the figures.

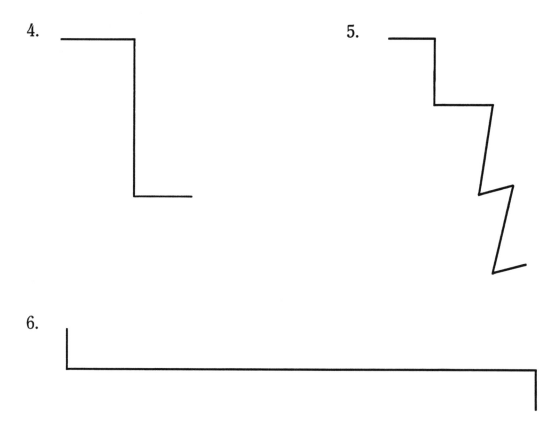

4.

5.

6.

Finding Perimeter

The perimeter of a shape is the distance around it. Find the perimeter of each shape below.

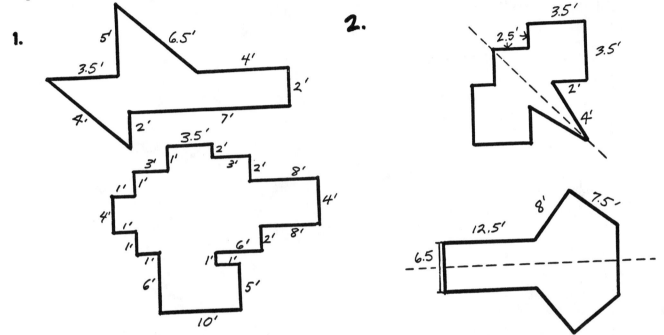

1.

2.

Assuming the following figures are drawn to scale, which shape from each set has the largest perimeter? Circle your choice.

A.

B.

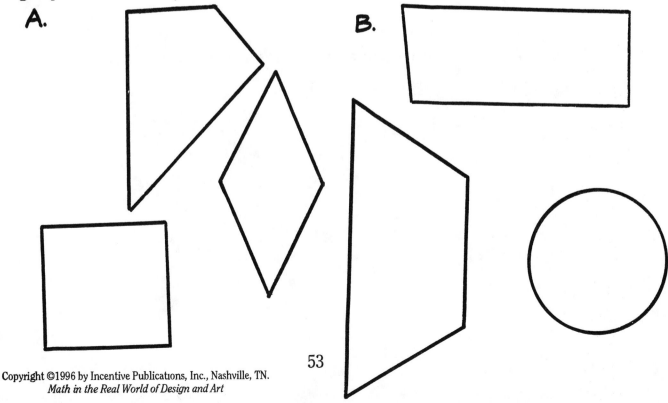

53

Exploring With Triangles

Cut a rectangle of construction paper into two right triangles. Using the two triangles, create as many different shapes as possible. Draw your shapes here:

Describe each of the shapes that you created and measure the perimeter of each one.

Which figure has the largest perimeter? Draw it here.

Advanced Perimeter Computations

Each of the polygons below comes with a specific set of measurements. Find the missing lengths, and then compute the perimeter of each shape.

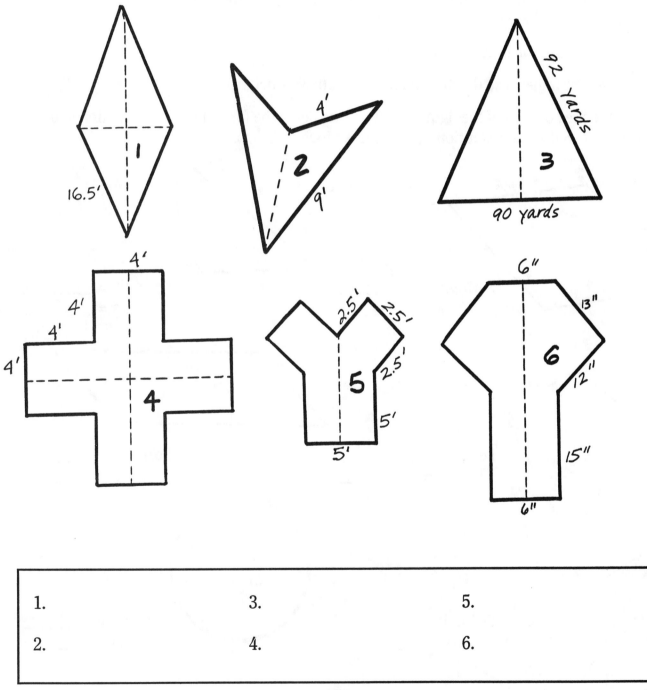

1.	3.	5.
2.	4.	6.

Computing Area

The area of a geometric shape is the floor space inside the shape. The area of different geometric shapes is found in different ways.

Square, rectangle, parallelogram: Multiply the length times the width to find the area inside these shapes.

Circles: Use the formula Area = πr^2

Right triangles: Use the formula A = $\frac{1}{2}$ bh (base x height)

Find the area of each of the figures below. Write down the formula you used to find your answer as well as your solution in the spaces provided below.

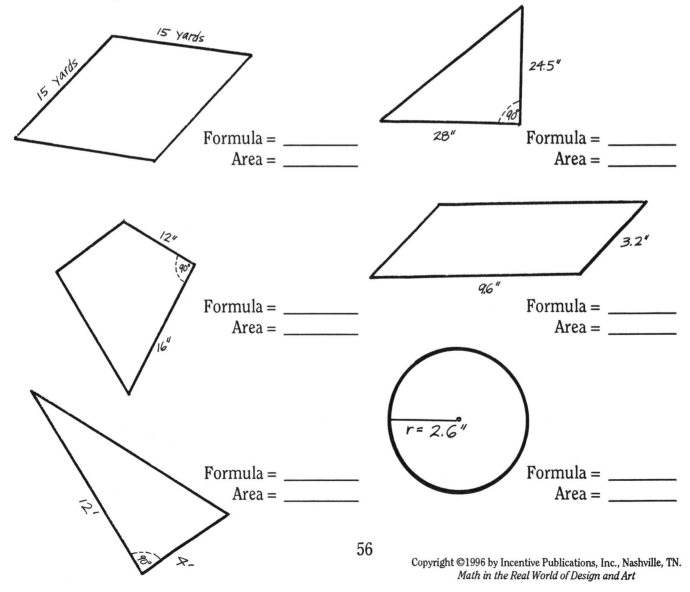

Formula = _____
Area = _____

Formula = _____
Area = _____

Formula = _____
Area = _____

Formula = _____
Area = _____

Formula = _____
Area = _____

Formula = _____
Area = _____

56

Area of Polygons

Polygons may be irregular in shape. To find the area of a polygon, you may wish to enclose the polygon in a rectangle and subtract all but the areas of the polygon from the area of the rectangle (Example A). You may also divide the contents of the polygon into units and half units and work from there (Example B).

Example A:

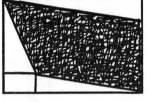

Example B:

Find the area of the polygons below.

1.

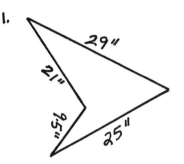

29"
21"
9.5"
25"

2.

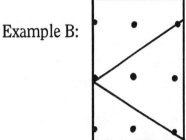

15'
24'
30'

3.

4.5"
9"
6.5"
9"
16"
8"

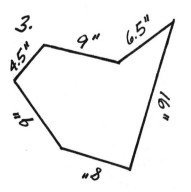

4.

24 yds.
19.6 yds.
24 yds.
29 yds.

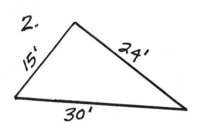

5.

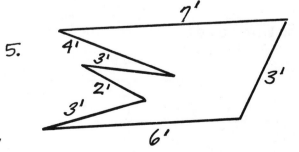

7'
4'
3'
3'
2'
3'
6'

Area

Putting a Price on the Area in Which You Live

If your home is rectangular, you can find its area by multiplying the length times the width. If your home has an irregular shape, you can find the area in a variety of ways. One way would be to divide the floorplan into parts, find the area of each separate part, and then add these numbers to get the total. What is another way to find the area of an irregular shape?

To find out how the square footage of a home and its price correlate, complete the following activity.
1. Go to the real estate section of a local newspaper.
2. Find four examples of homes that are about the same number of square feet. Be sure the price of each home is listed.
3. Determine the price per square foot for each home. What formula will you use? List each price per square foot below:

Home 1   Home 2

Home 3   Home 4

4. How do the per-square-foot prices compare? _____

_____

_____

5. What could be some reasons for differences in per-square-foot prices? _____

_____

_____

58

The Great Display

During several different months of the school year, collectors have been invited to display their collections on one of the walls of your classroom. Help them determine the number of pieces from their collection that they will be able to display based on the area available on your wall. The height of the wall is eight feet, and the width is fifteen feet. There is a window in the center of the wall that is four feet by six feet.

October: Your teacher is friends with a great baseball card collector. If each baseball card in the collection is 3.5 inches tall and 2.5 inches wide, how many cards can be displayed on one wall of your classroom?

Show your work here:

January: A famous coin collector is coming to your classroom. She will display her world class quarter collection. How many quarters will she be able to display on one wall of your classroom?

Show your work here:

March: Your teacher has a huge collection of billed caps. If each hat has a diameter of about 7 inches when the bill is flipped up, how many hats can be displayed on one wall of your classroom?

Show your work here:

Three-Dimensional Shapes

When a geometric shape has depth and width and height, it is three-dimensional. A shoe box is a good example of a three-dimensional geometric shape. What are some others?

Problem: Using marshmallows and toothpicks, how many three-dimensional shapes can you create? Draw each shape as you create it.

Answer the following questions.

1. What is the strongest three-dimensional geometric structure that you created? _____

2. How long (in toothpick lengths) is the longest three-dimensional structure that you created? _____

3. How high (in toothpick lengths) is the highest three-dimensional structure that you created? _____

4. What is the smallest three-dimensional geometric structure that you created? _____

5. Draw your most unique three-dimensional geometric structure below:

Math in the Real World of Design and Art

Investigating Solids

A solid is a three-dimensional figure with height, width, and length. One example of a solid is a cube.

Complete the following activities:

1. Cut and fold several of the patterns available from your teacher. Before you begin your cutting and folding process, predict what you believe each shape will look like.

    A. Pattern Number_____ Predicted Shape:

    B. Pattern Number_____ Predicted Shape:

    C. Pattern Number_____ Predicted Shape:

2 To find the volume of a three-dimensional shape, use the formula v = lwh (volume = length x width x height). As volume is the cubic space found in three-dimensional objects, volume is three-dimensional.

    Find the volume of each object below:

    D. Your whirlpool tub is 6 feet long, 4 feet wide, and 2½ feet deep. What is its volume?

    E. Your family wants to create a new duck pond in the backyard. It will be 27 feet long and 14 feet wide. The average depth of the pond will be 6 feet. How many gallons of water will it take to fill the pond? (*Hint: There are about 7.48 gallons of water in a cubic foot.)

Pattern #1

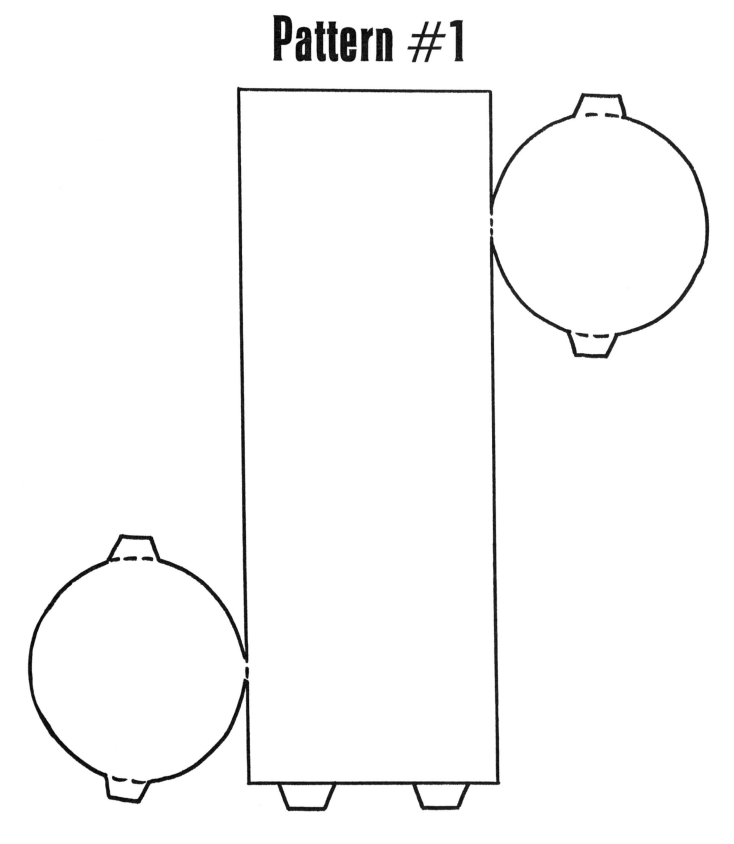

Pattern #2

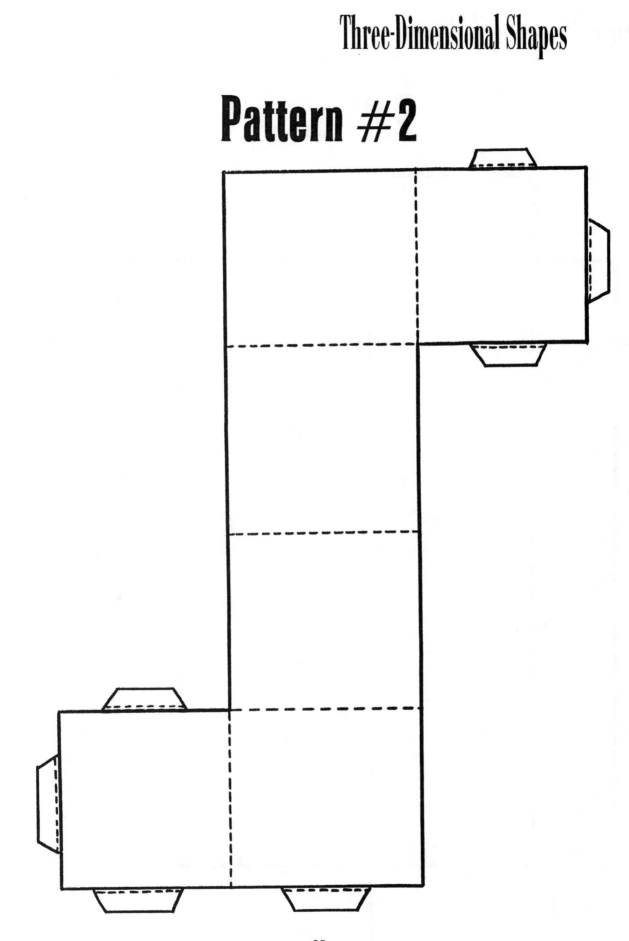

Math in the Real World of Design and Art

Pattern #3

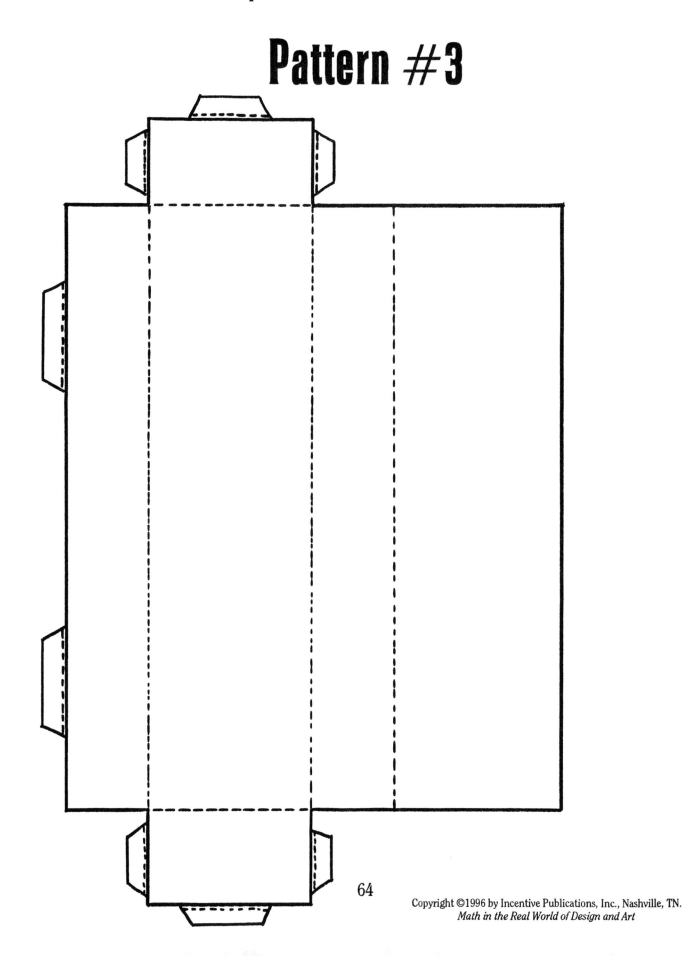

Pattern #4

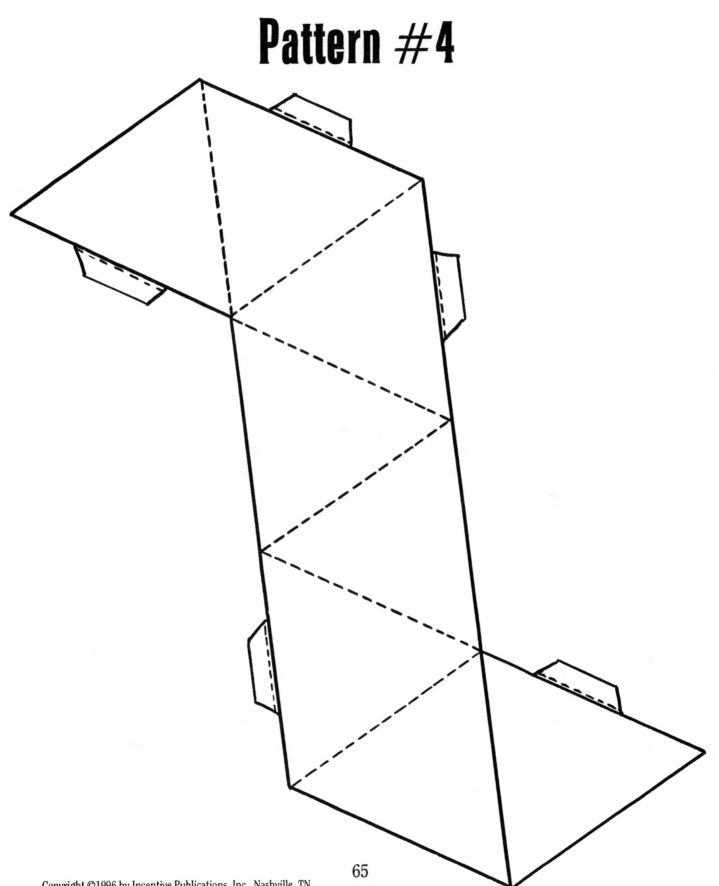

65

Pattern #5

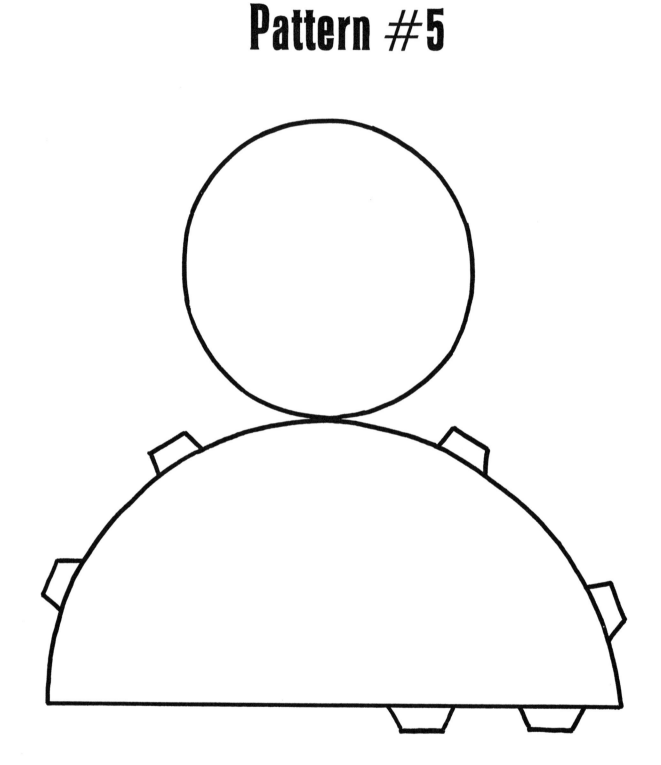

66

Pattern #6

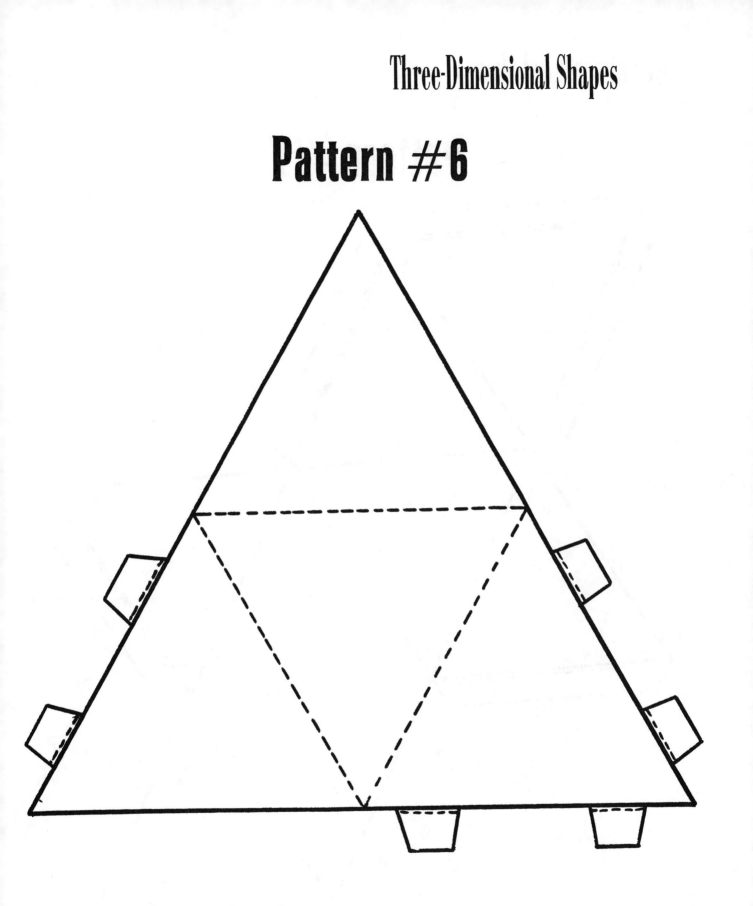

Pattern #7

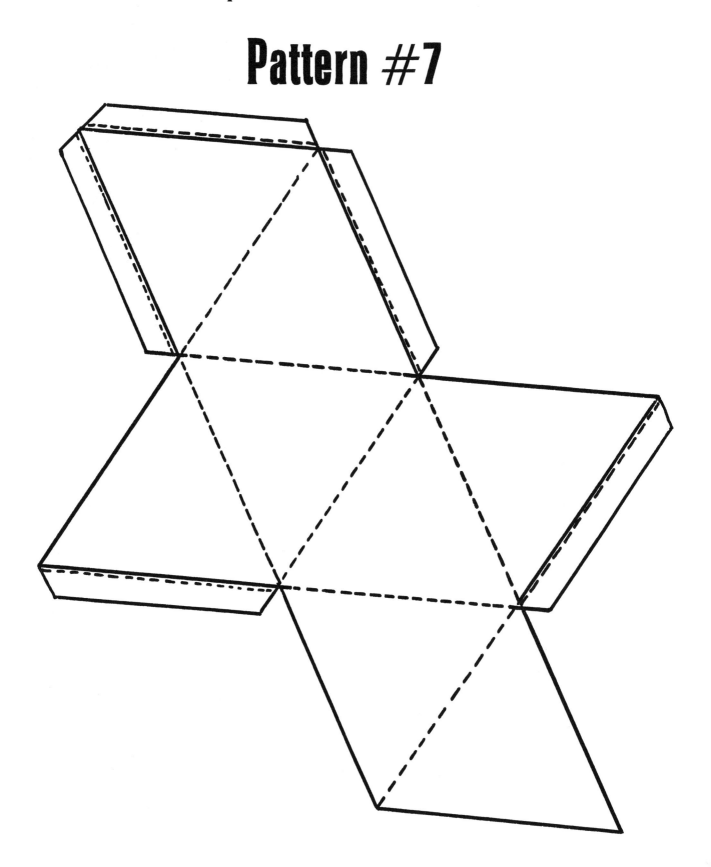

Pattern #8

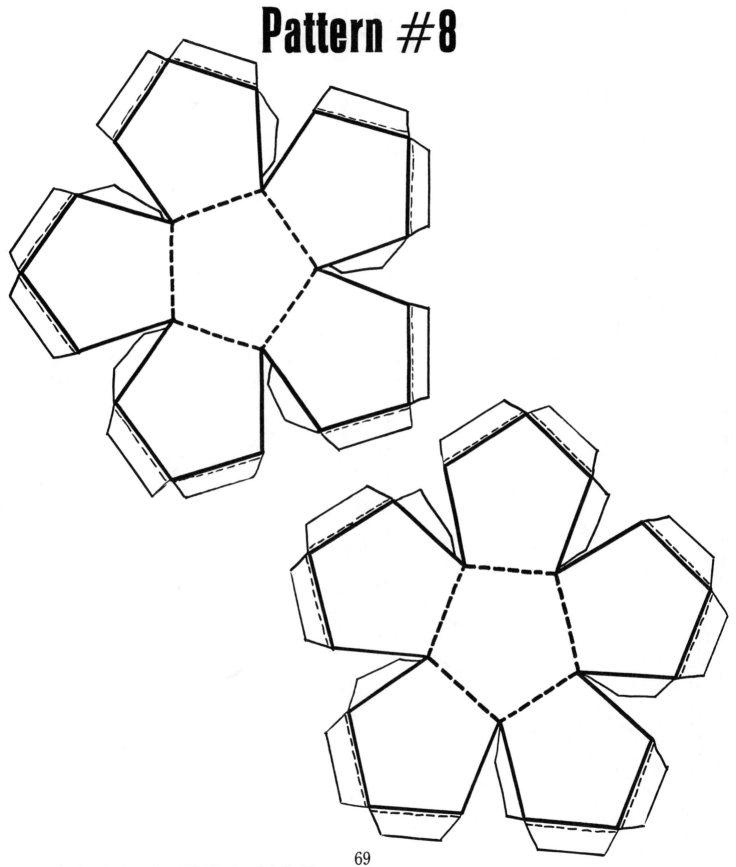

The Octahedron

Trace the pattern shown below twice. Cut out both shapes and use them to create an octahedron. (Join two identical pyramids.)

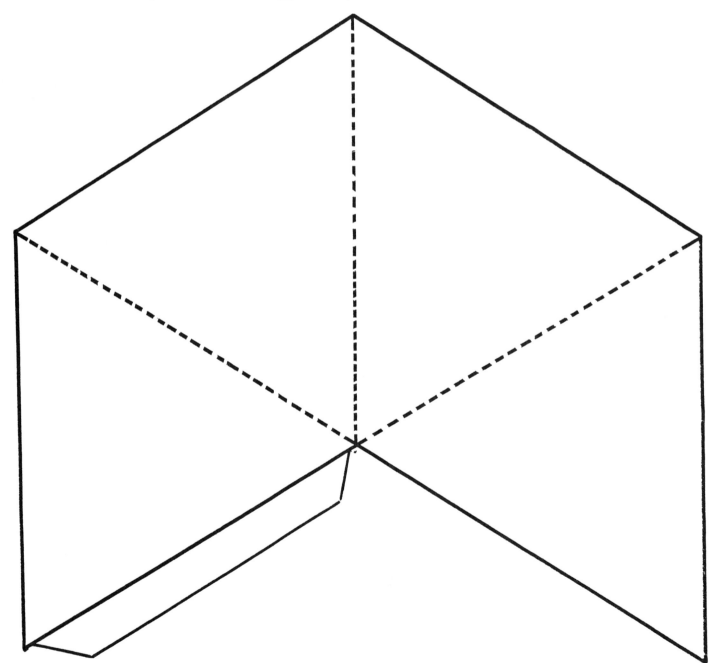

70

The Stellated Dodecahedron

Use twelve of the pattern shown to create a starlike dodecahedron. Make one pyramid and attach five more around its base. Create a second such group and join the two.

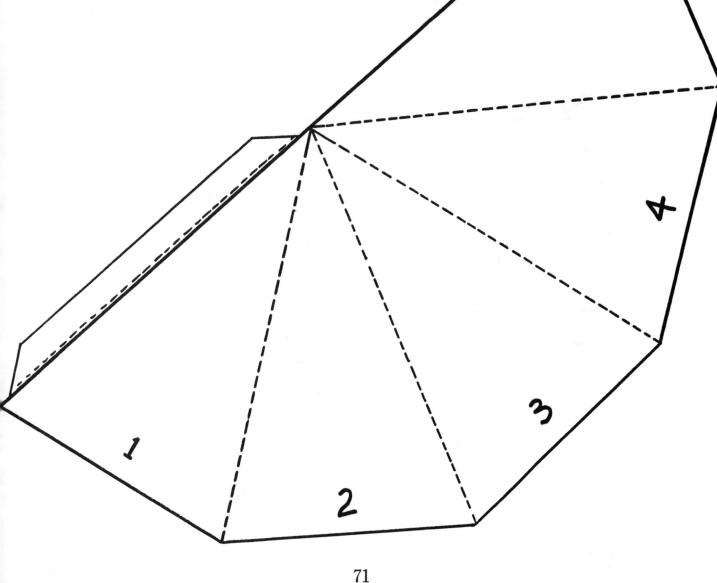

The Icosahedron

Twenty equilateral triangles make up the icosahedron. First make a group of ten. Then make a second group of ten and join the two.

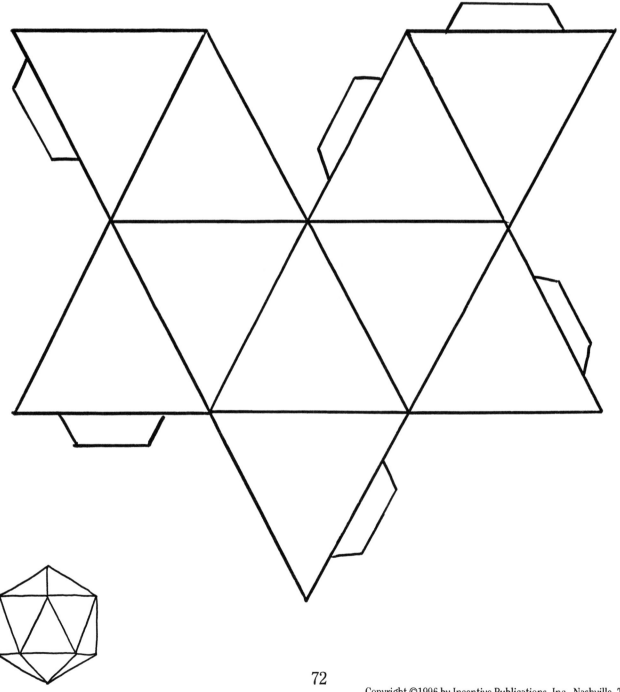

The Pentagonal Dodecahedron

This figure is made up of twelve identical five-sided pentagons. Make two of the pattern, and join them together.

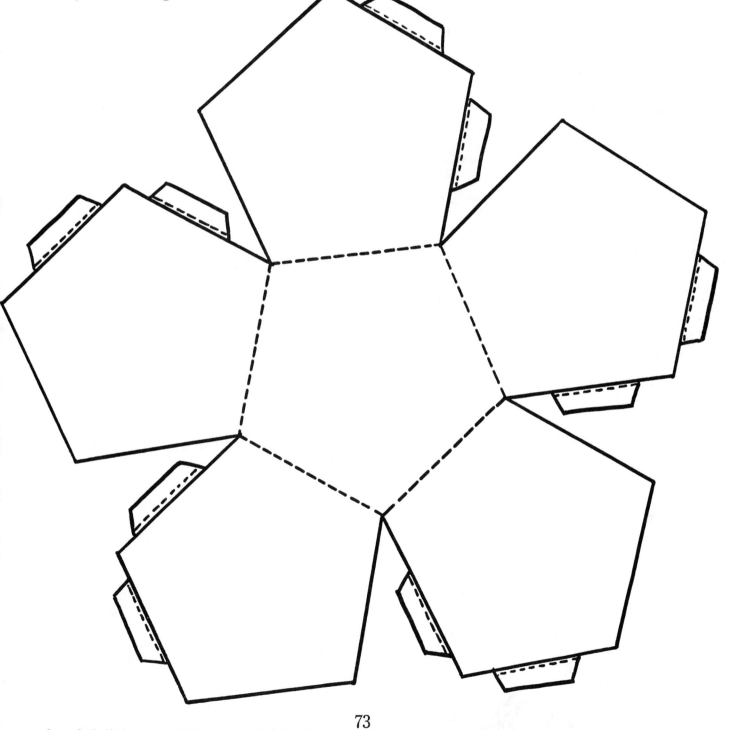

Volume and Cylinders

Remember that the volume of a cube is found by taking the length times the width and multiplying that answer by the height. To find the volume of a cylinder, we use the formula $V = \pi r^2 h$. Since a cylinder has a circular end, we first find the area of the circle. Then we multiply that number times the depth.

Find the volume of the following containers.

1. You have a can of soda that is 5 inches high. The top of the soda can is shown below.

   Show your work here:

   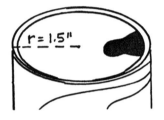

   What is the volume of the can? _____

2. An oil company has just ordered a new storage tank for petroleum. The tank is 36 feet long and has a diameter of 20 feet. What is the volume of the tank?

3. If one cubic foot can hold 7.48 gallons, how many gallons can the tank in question two hold?

4. Water is running through the garden hose when it is suddenly stopped. The hose is 42 feet long and has a diameter of 3 inches. If the hose is completely filled with water, how much water can it hold?

Math in the Real World of Design and Art

Face the Facts

Complete the chart below.

SHAPE	NUMBER OF VERTICES	NUMBER OF FACES	NUMBER OF EDGES
1. Cube			
2. Prism			
3. Cylinder			
4. Pyramid			
5. Octahedron			
6. Icosahedron			
7. Stellated Dodecahedron			
8. Pentagonal Dodecahedron			

75

Mystery Shapes

Read the information given about each shape. Use up to twenty cubes to construct each shape according to the directions that are given. Draw each shape as you create it.

1. Use fifteen cubes to make a solid shape that is two layers tall. Draw it here.

2. Use ten cubes to make a solid shape that is three layers tall. Draw it here.

3. Use twenty cubes to make a solid shape that is four layers tall. Draw your shape here.

4. Combine your cubes with a partner or two. Create a shape that is four or more layers tall. Use as many cubes as you need to use to create a box. Draw it here.

5. What is the smallest cube, using more than one cube, that you can create? Draw it here.

6. Draw your most unusual shape here. Describe it.

Believe It or Not!

The average can is approximately 5 inches tall and has a diameter of 2½ inches. According to research conducted in 1990, the average American uses 1500 cans per year.

Take a survey of at least twenty people that you know. Ask them to give you the approximate number of cans that they think they use in a typical day. (You should include all types of cans—fruits, vegetables, soda, spaghetti, etc.)

Use one of the graph forms provided in the back of this book and project the number of cans each of these individuals uses in a year's period of time.

Compare the information you collected in your original research to the information gathered in the 1990 research. Write a brief news report below to share your findings.

_____

_____

_____

_____

_____

_____

_____

_____

_____

_____

Bonus: If the national average is actually close to 1500 cans per person per year, what would be the average number of gallons of food and drink that would be consumed if a typical can is 5 inches tall and has a diameter of 2½"? (Remember: there are 7.48 gallons in a cubic foot.)

Three-Dimensional Tic-Tac-Toe

Use the game board below to play a three-dimensional form of tic-tac-toe. The playing cube is composed of four layers of smaller cubes. With a partner, take turns placing your X or O on any cube in any layer. The first player to get four Xs or Os in a row horizontally, vertically, or diagonally in any one layer or through any four, is the winner.

78

Designing a Geo-Lab

Planning Log

Name: _____

The Geo-Lab

Your company has been hired to build your school district's first Geo-Lab. The lab will become a place for students interested in becoming better mathematicians to go to work on real-life applications of math. In the Geo-Lab there will be a state-of-the-art computer lab, an area designed for larger scale construction when solving problems, a kitchen area, several work stations for individuals and small groups, five large classrooms equipped with laboratory facilities, and a reference library.

Your company must construct a scale model of the lab to display their vision of how the lab will look. Of course, since it is a Geo-Lab, it must be built entirely of geometric forms. The model must be built to scale and must include all of the areas described in the first paragraph.

Your company must make a presentation of its final product to the prospective buyers. This presentation should include:

1. Rationale and support for the design
2. Cost analysis
3. Explanation of special features
4. Display of model and accompanying brochure
5. Carefully planned sales talk

During the time that your company is in business, you will all need to assume responsibility for getting the necessary work accomplished. Some of the things that you will need to do include to:

1. Determine a reasonable amount of money to spend per square foot for the construction of the building. Try to stay within your budget.
2. Determine the jobs of the team members. Remember that everyone needs to stay on track, remain focused, attend to quality control so that all jobs are done neatly, and take care of construction supplies.
3. Decide on a way to determine how decisions will be made in the event that there are differences of opinion.
4. Make sure that your cleanup is successful each day. Your company will be fined if anyone has to do any outside cleanup ($1,000 per cleanup).
5. Set goals for each day so that your project can be completed within the amount of time specified by your teacher.

Your Geo-Lab will be constructed of newspaper dowels. Each dowel will be constructed by the team from a half sheet of newspaper rolled diagonally.

The dowels will be held together with tape or staples. The structure must be entirely freestanding in its completed form. Tape will cost you $10 per inch. You will need to estimate the approximate amount that your team uses.

Each sheet of newspaper may be purchased from your teacher for $400. Each full sheet will make two dowels. The dowels will be cut into halves and smaller units as needed for your construction.

Your company will also be allowed to use rulers, pencils, and glue. The basic structure of the building will be the focus of your team. You will not need to show interior walls or any of the furnishings. However, you will need to create a blueprint of the floorplan. This blueprint will be done to scale and will include all of the areas mentioned at the beginning of your journal.

Your company will need to accurately present square footage information to the prospective buyers. As a bonus, you may wish to see if you can determine the volume of your building.

At the end of each day, write a brief evaluation of the way things went with the design team and any other questions or comments. Be sure to include things that went well along with areas that may need improvement. Suggest ideas to help facilitate that improvement.

In the area below, sketch the way that you think the Geo-Lab might look. Remember to include area for the rooms defined at the onset of the project and to keep the form entirely geometric.

Lesson 2 GEO-LAB

Get together with the members of your team. Compare drawings from Lesson 1. Work together to create a design that satisfies everyone. Sketch your final design here:

You will be using the scale of ¼ inch equals 1 foot. Find a way to determine how many dowels you think your team will need for its construction. **You will be able to purchase dowels only three times.** Make sure that you work as accurately as possible to determine the number of dowels you think you will need for your construction. (Your construction will be judged on originality, structural sturdiness, special features, and appropriateness for the task.)

Show your work here:

Evaluation of the day's work: _____

_____

_____

_____

_____

Today you will make your purchases and begin your construction. Each member of the team should have responsibility for a portion of the work—making dowels, keeping expense records, measuring and cutting dowels, taping, stapling, or gluing dowels together, working on the blueprint of the interior floor space, designing special features, etc.

As a team, discuss the responsibilities of each member. Compare Expense Logs with your company members as you work to see if you have recorded your expenses accurately. You will have $15,000 to spend.

Expense Log

Date	Item Purchased	Amount Spent	Amount Remaining

Begin construction of your Geo-Lab.

Evaluation of the day's work: _____

_____

_____

_____

_____

Continue working on the construction of the Geo-Lab's exterior structure.

Create a pencil sketch of a special feature that you would like to include in the lab. Briefly tell why you feel it would be a selling feature of the lab.

Description of special feature: _____

_____

_____

_____

_____

Evaluation of the day's work: _____

_____

_____

_____

_____

Lesson 5 GEO-LAB

You should begin the finishing stages of the Geo-Lab's exterior construction.

Begin to meet with your team members to design a blueprint of the floorplan.

Sketch the blueprint you agree upon here. Determine the square footage and record it here.

Evaluation of the day's work: _____

_____

_____

_____

You should finish your exterior structure today. Write a TV or radio advertisement for your finished product here:

If you were to advertise your product in a newspaper or magazine, what would your visual ad look like? Design it here.

Evaluation of the day's work: _____

_____

_____

_____

_____

Today you should be putting together your classroom sales presentation. You will need to:

1. Decide on what each member of the team will do and say.
2. Create a brochure to advertise your product. Each member of the team should add something to the brochure. You can do a tri-fold brochure by folding a sheet of typing paper accordion style into three parts, a bi-fold brochure by folding the paper in half, or a one-page brochure. Make your brochure colorful and inviting. Make sure to advertise your most important pieces of information.
3. Finalize your Expense Log.
4. Evaluate your project.

Project Evaluation Checklist

Please rate each of the following statements . . . 5 (Strongly Agree), 3 (Agree), 1 (Disagree)

	5	3	1
1. I am pleased with our team's final project.	5	3	1
2. Our team worked well together.	5	3	1
3. I became a better problem solver during the project.	5	3	1
4. We had a difficult time agreeing.	5	3	1
5. Everyone participated equally.	5	3	1
6. I was a cooperative group member.	5	3	1
7. I understand everything that we did.	5	3	1
8. The project was too difficult.	5	3	1

Comments: _____

_____

_____

_____

_____

_____

_____

Name _____ Date _____

TITLE OF GRAPH _____

Key ⬜ _____

TITLE OF GRAPH _____ **Name** _____ **Date** _____

Key ☐

90

Name _____ Date _____

TITLE OF GRAPH _____

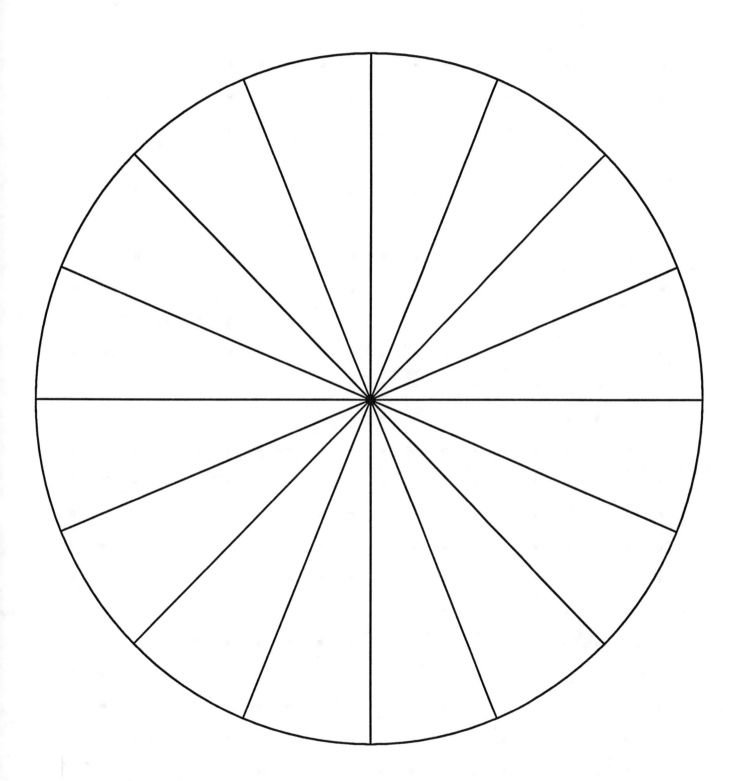

Key ⬜ _____

Math in the Real World of Design and Art

Square Dot Paper Grid Master

Square Dot Paper Grid Master

1/4" Graph Paper

$1/_2$ " Graph Paper

1 " Graph Paper